SIMPLICITY AND PURITY

READING GANDHI IN TWO TONGUES

Studies in Comparative Literature
Jadavpur University

Studies in Comparative Literature, Jadavpur University, is founded on the view that the study of literatures and the arts in multilingual and culturally diverse contexts such as India demands a comparative approach. It is informed by an interdisciplinary and intercultural focus on bhasha literatures, translation, orality and performance as well as other arts and digital humanities, in the context of local, national and international literary and cultural transactions. The series is meant for students, scholars, and teachers of comparative literature as well as of single literature and other humanities departments. It brings together the work of faculty members and scholars at the Department of Comparative Literature, Jadavpur University, as well as of national and international visiting scholars who have enriched its research and debates.

Sub-series I: Texts, Contexts, Methods

Ia. Histories and Paradigms
Ib. Approaching New Challenges, Recasting Paradigms

Sub-series II: Indian and Asian Contexts

Sub-series III: Literature and Other Knowledge Systems

IIIa. Literary Studies and Performance
IIIb. Literature and Indigenous Knowledge Systems

Sub-series IV: Lecture Series

Contributions based on talks by Visiting Scholars

STUDIES IN COMPARATIVE LITERATURE
JADAVPUR UNIVERSITY

SUB-SERIES IV: LECTURES

SIMPLICITY AND PURITY

Poets, Farmers and Parsis
of Gandhi's Gujarati

❖ ❖ ❖

READING GANDHI IN TWO TONGUES

Tridip Suhrud

Orient BlackSwan

SIMPLICITY AND PURITY; READING GANDHI IN TWO TONGUES

ORIENT BLACKSWAN PRIVATE LIMITED

Registered Office
3-6-752 Himayatnagar, Hyderabad 500 029, Telangana, India
E-mail: centraloffice@orientblackswan.com

Other Offices
Bengaluru, Chennai, Guwahati, Hyderabad, Kolkata,
Mumbai, New Delhi, Noida, Patna

First published 2023

041725

ISBN 978-93-5442-360-4

Typeset in Adobe Garamond Pro 12.5/15.6 *by*
Shine Graphics, Delhi 110 094

Printed at
Avantika Printers Private Limited, New Delhi 110020

Published by
Orient Blackswan Private Limited
3-6-752, Himayatnagar, Hyderabad 500 029, Telangana, India
E-mail: info@orientblackswan.com

Contents

General Introduction

The first full-fledged department of Comparative Literature in India, and the second in Asia, was established in Calcutta at Jadavpur University in 1956. The reputed Bangla poet, writer and scholar Buddhadeva Bose was its founder and the first Head of the Department. The *Jadavpur Journal of Comparative Literature*, launched here in 1961, is one of the oldest journals in Asia that has continued, regularly, to publish significant research in comparative literature by national and international scholars. In the late 1980s the UGC earmarked the department for promotion of teaching and research under its Special Assistance Programme. In the early nineties the department widened its areas of interest to first introduce courses in the literatures and cultures of Bangladesh, Africa, Canada and Latin America; then it set up centres in the latter three, subsequently a Centre for Translation of Indian Literatures, and, most recently, a Centre for Studies of Islamicate Asia. During the Tenth Plan the department was also selected by the UGC to participate in its ASIHSS (Assistance for Strengthening of Infrastructure for Humanities and Social Sciences) programme. In addition to these UGC programmes and these centres, the UPE—University with Potential for Excellence—programme of the UGC also enabled the establishment of research projects in the department. These included translation and intercultural studies under Project Anuvad; documentation and research relating to performers of traditional dramatic forms in different districts of West Bengal under Project Palagaan; and a unique new venture involving an exploration of Kolkata through narratives of sound under the project Soundscapes. The first and so far only UGC Centre of Advanced Study in Comparative Literature in India was also established in this department in 2005, and it continued promoting research into its current phase. This series, Studies in Comparative Literature, Jadavpur University, is rooted in this academic history of over six decades.

When other departments of Comparative Literature finally began to be established in India in the 1990s, a sharing of our research and pedagogic experience became imperative. As the practice of comparative literature proliferated in centres and newly established departments as well as in single literature departments right across India, we began to face persistent requests for enhanced access to our research from academics, researchers and students alike. Our research, while considerable, had largely been published by local presses and the university, and did not have the national outreach now demanded of it. It was in response to this need that the idea of initiating a series with a reputed mainstream national publisher came about, and we are especially happy about this partnership with Orient BlackSwan, given the important role it has played in the dissemination of scholarship on Indian literatures and cultures.

We hold that the study of literatures and the arts in multilingual and culturally diverse countries such as ours demands a comparative approach; hence, Studies in Comparative Literature, Jadavpur University, is a series for students, scholars and teachers of comparative literature as well as of single literature, arts and other humanities departments. It explores a range of histories, theoretical reflections, as well as innovative approaches and concerns relevant to the field of comparative literature. In keeping with the basic imperatives of comparative literature, it is both intercultural and interdisciplinary in that it engages with the trajectories of literatures across cultures as well as with the relations between literatures and other fields of creative expression. It is thus informed by an interdisciplinary and intercultural focus on *bhasha* literatures, translation, orality and performance as well as other arts and digital humanities, in the context of local, national and international literary and cultural transactions, and also those of the borderlands.

This series brings together the work of faculty and scholars at the department of Comparative Literature, Jadavpur University, and of national and international visiting scholars. It comprises both edited volumes and authored books, as well as monographs by visiting scholars. The series launches the research carried out under the third phase of the UGC Centre of Advanced Study in Comparative Literature, and the publication of these volumes, we hope, will mark the beginnings of a renewed mapping of comparative literary studies in India.

The current studies build on the foundations of creative intellectual vision, innovative pedagogy and several decades of original scholarship that went into the shaping of what was a new field of study, in fact a new mode of inquiry, in the Indian university. Many generations have enriched comparative literary studies in India, and it is impossible to chart all the contributions of even just those at the Department of Comparative Literature at Jadavpur University in the space of a short introduction such as this. What follows however is a brief account of the directions of research, and of the kinds of publications that emerged from this research, as well as in response to pedagogic needs at this department; it is being presented here as an academic contextualisation for the present series that may be useful to other scholars, centres and departments of not just comparative literature but also literary studies in general.

Before mapping the broad areas of research across the decades however, it may be relevant to reflect for a moment on the intellectual and creative range of teachers and scholars who contributed to its making. Buddhadeva Bose and Sudhindranath Dutta were towering modern Bangla poets and writers, and amongst the foremost intellectuals of their time. Joining them in the early years were Fr. Robert Antoine, a Belgian Jesuit priest who was a Sanskritist and a scholar of Greek and Latin, who translated Kalidasa's *Raghuvamsa* from the Sanskrit into English, and also collaborated on a translation of Virgil's *Aeneid* from the Latin into Bangla; Fr. Pierre Fallon, who was also a Belgian Jesuit priest, a professor of French literature, a licenciate in philosophy and theology and an expert in Bangla philology; and David J. McCutchion who had trained in French and German at Jesus College Cambridge, and later became an authority on both the terracotta temples as well as the *patuas* (scroll painters) of Bengal. The next two generations of teacher-scholars, five of whom also trained in M.A. or Ph.D. programmes of North American departments of Comparative Literature and others in France or Germany, included Naresh Guha, Amiya Dev, Deepak Mazumdar, Subir Roychowdhury, Swapan Mazumdar, Bijoya Das, Subha Chakraborty Dasgupta, Ipsita Chanda, Suman Ghosh, Alokeranjan Dasgupta, Pranabendu Dasgupta, Manabendra Bandyopadhyay, Nabaneeta Dev Sen, Sibaji Bandyopadhyay and Debiprasad Bhattacharya. All of them earned international repute as scholars, and while the last was a polyglot and a renowned Sanskritist, the penultimate five were also major creative writers in Bangla.

It is perhaps the wide range of exposure and training, which was as rigorous as it may seem eclectic, that cautioned scholars of this department about strait-jacketing comparative literary studies into any definitive 'school' or methodology, or of limiting Indian literary studies within the political borders of the Indian nation state. So, even in their pioneering role, they refrained from formulating a Jadavpur 'school' of Comparative Literature, or privileging any comparative methodology over others. They also desisted from confining literary studies to inter-Indian literary relations only, and conscientiously trained their lenses on the wider South-Asian and Asian, Perso-Arabic and Anglo-European fields too; and eventually they reached out to Latin America, Africa and Australia, especially in relation to transactions with Indian literatures and cultures, but also otherwise. Such catholicity, in both approach and range, would naturally give rise to questions of delimitation and focus—and what emerges clearly as a connecting thread across the decades is that, in terms of both literary-cultural focus and methodological approach, scholars here responded to the ground realities and the needs of their times.

It was in the early 1990s that the consolidated programme of publishing started, supported by the Special Assistance Programme of the UGC; the focus in this decade was clearly on creating resources for research. Bibliographies of reception—of World Literature in Bangla periodicals, and of Bangla literature in South Indian languages—formed one thrust area. Translation became a focal point from the beginning: translation of material such as literary manifestoes in Indian languages, and discussions regarding the aesthetics as well as comparative literature methodologies of translation featured in this phase. Literary historiography in India featured as an important concern as did East–West literary interactions of the colonial period. The fourth area of concern was in relation to third-world contexts—to cultures of silence as well as the challenge of envisioning their futures—and this included reflection on African and Latin American literatures and cultures.

The focus on generating resources for comparative research continued through the next five years with translations across several genres (poetry, short stories, plays and excerpts of autobiographies) and several languages (that is, from Bangla into other languages such as Asamiya and English, and from Odia, Gujarati, Marathi and other Indian languages into English as well as Bangla). Also, the first phase had documented debates on comparative literary approaches to historiography; this one brought into focus issues of genology from a comparative perspective, with a volume tracing the *charit* as a genre. A third area of engagement was that of linguistic and cultural formations of self-identity across the literatures of Bengal and Bangladesh, thus bringing the literature of Bangladesh into the purview of our research. This phase was also marked by the publication of three volumes under the rubric of Literary Studies in India: on Literary Historiography, Thematology and Genology; it brought together reflections of comparative literature academics as well as scholars from other literature and humanities departments, on approaches to literary studies in India at the beginning of the twenty-first century.

In the first phase of the Centre of Advanced Study (2005–2010), we continued, on the one hand with the task of generating resources for research, such as the annotated bibliography of Bangla and Asamiya histories of literature;

on the other hand we extended the work on historiography to specific areas of study such as Indian English literature. Two new sets of concerns came into focus in this period. One set related to the need to document and study the fast-disappearing body of folk performances—the outcomes included the recordings and studies of *Manasamangal pala* and *Banabibir pala.* The other set of concerns was underlined by the realisation that most of our international focus had been on literary relations with the Anglo-European world, while those with other Asian cultures had not received the attention they deserved; thus the imperative to retrieve and explore these resulted in a focus on travel literature from Asia with focus on the collection of literary material along sea and trade routes, and the publication of a bibliography of travelogues to Asian countries in Bangla as well as an anthology of Bangla and Odia writings on colonial Burma. During this phase the additional support from the Assistance for Strengthening of Infrastructure for Humanities and Social Sciences (ASIHSS) programme of the UGC enabled research in South Asian contexts and resulted in the publication of a South Asian nationalisms reader, as well as a volume on the poetics and politics of Sufism and Bhakti in South Asia.

The following years, in the second phase of the CAS, were marked by more extensive and deeperresearch in the fields already marked out. At least three areas that had clearly emerged as thrust areas were:

- Comparative Literature: Explorations in Discipline and Methodology
- Roots and Routes: Intra-Indian and Intra-Asian Linguistic, Literary and Cultural Relations
- Literature and Other Knowledge Systems

Resources generated for research during this period included a handbook on terms and concepts in comparative literature, a volume on comparative literature in Germany, and textbooks on Indian Nepali literature in English and Bangla. The publications on comparative explorations in genre included a study of the *namah*. Research on folk cultures as knowledge systems resulted in publications on *charak* and *gajan* in Bengal, another on Karbi oral traditions in the Northeast, as well as a volume on literatures and oratures as knowledge systems, based on texts from Northeast India. A comparative study on the *ghumantoo* roadies, or wanderers, of India and Canada added to this set. In the context of Asian studies, research was published on tales of medieval China. The research on South Asia extended itself to comparative studies of the literatures and cultures of borders in South Asia and the Americas; this last volume marked entry into a new area of research—Comparative Border Studies.

The present series has been envisioned as follows:

Studies in Comparative Literature, Jadavpur University

Sub-series I: Texts, Contexts, Methods

1a. Histories and Paradigms
1b. Approaching New Challenges, Recasting Paradigms

Sub-series II: Indian and Asian Contexts

Sub-series III: Literature and Other Knowledge Systems

IIIa. Literary Studies and Performance
IIIb. Literature and Indigenous Knowledge Systems

Sub-series IV: Lecture Series

Contributions based on talks by Visiting Scholars

In many ways it marks a deepening and consolidation of perspectives across the earlier decades of research; in other ways it also charts new directions in comparative literary studies. The sub-series **Texts, Contexts, Methods** includes two histories in the section *Histories and Paradigms*—one of the emergence and establishment of Indian Comparative Literature, the other a disciplinary and institutional history of comparative literature in India, based on documents preserved at Jadavpur as well as gathered from across the country. Planned along with these are anthologies on texts, contexts and concepts, and on comparative literary studies in India, with contributions from scholars across the country. The section *Approaching New Challenges, Recasting Paradigms* will introduce research in new directions that responds to contemporary challenges. Comparative Literature as a discipline has historically crossed borders in terms of time and space. One of these volumes is a response to the now pervasive trans-national histories of migrants and refugees and, focussing on the Indo-Bangladesh border, it marks a shift from the prism of the 'national' to the prism of borders and frontiers, to the epistemological perspectives of 'borderlanders'; another volume charts the transformations in comparative literary studies in light of the mutual interactions between digital humanities and literary mapping in South Asia.

The sub-series **Indian and Asian Contexts** includes both intra-Indian literary translations and a mapping of linguistic, literary and cultural relations grouped under the rubric of *Roots and Routes*, as well as translations from Bangla and Urdu of fictional and discursive writings of Muslim literati in Bengal from the early twentieth century onward. Included in this sub-series are comparative studies of 'progressive' literatures, South Asian studies of transnational writers such as Ismat Chughtai, and studies of intra-Asian engagements such as Bengal's encounters with Japan in the twentieth century.

The third sub-series, **Literature and Other Knowledge Systems**, includes a volume on reflections on methodology in the translation of performance texts in the sub-section *Literary Studies and Performance*; the sub-section on *Literature and Indigenous Knowledge Systems* carries a comparative study of Karbi and Chakma narrative traditions of Northeast India, as well as another of creation songs from India, Canada, Australia and Southeast Asia.

Finally, the **Lecture Series** comprises volumes based on talks delivered by national and international visiting scholars who have enriched the research and debates of our department, and often taken us in new directions too. We are truly grateful to Alessandro Portelli, Professor Emeritus, University of Rome La Sapienza, and Tridip Suhrud, Professor and Provost, CEPT University, Ahmedabad, for their contributions on oral history and Gandhi's languages respectively, and for their generosity in permitting us to include earlier landmark essays in their volumes. We also extend our gratitude to Robert P Goldman, Professor, University of California at Berkeley, and Daniel Rycroft, Associate Professor at the University of East Anglia for having agreed to write for us on the Valmiki *Ramayana* and the humanities in India, respectively. We thank other scholars, who have collaborated in the research on some of our publications; they include Jatin Nayak, former Professor of Utkal University, Indranil Acharya, Professor at Vidyasagar University, Subha Chakraborty Dasgupta former Professor in our own department, Shraddhanjali Tamang, also a faculty member at Jadavpur University, and writer Manoranjan Byapari.

This series is the collaborative effort of all the faculty members of the Comparative Literature department: Suchorita Chattopadhyay, Kunal Chattopadhyay, Aveek Majumder, Sayantan Dasgupta, Sujit Kumar Mandal, Parthasarathi Bhaumik, Epsita Halder, Debashree Dattaray and Sumit Kumar Barua. They have been working concertedly towards its publication over the last several years; and while the individual volumes will carry their respective names as authors, editors and co-authors, it needs to be put on record that this series is finally seeing the light of day through one of the most devastating pandemics in history only because of their determined collective commitment and mutual intellectual inspiration. We are also grateful to our research fellows—who will be acknowledged individually in the respective volumes—for their selfless and cheerful support. Last but not least we extend our deep gratitude to Padmaja Anant of Orient BlackSwan for her wisdom and infinite patience—it has indeed been a pleasure working with her.

KAVITA PANJABI
SAMANTAK DAS
SUCHETA BHATTACHARYA
Series Editors

The first volumes of this series are being sent to the press with a heavy heart, for Samantak Das is with us no more. May the infallible spirit with which he contributed to the making of this series continue to enrich it in the years to come.

Simplicity and Purity: Poets, Farmers and Parsis of Gandhi's Gujarati

On 31 October 1936, M. K. Gandhi presided over the twelfth annual meeting of the Gujarati Sahitya Parishad, a body of litterateurs that was formed in the first decade of the twentieth century. The body that formally came into existence in 1905 elected Govardhanram Tripathi, the writer of a four-part novel *Sarasvatichandra* that Gandhi had read and admired and whose impact on intellectual and social life of Gujarat he was well aware of, as its first president. From 1928 till 1955 K. M. Munshi was the de facto president of the Parishad.

It was Munshi who had persuaded Gandhi to accept to be the president for the twelfth session. Gandhi required to be 'persuaded.' In 1925 he had resolutely declined this responsibility and in August 1919 he had been defeated in his attempt to become the president of the Sahitya Parishad. The literary class of Gujarat at that point preferred a former officer of the Baroda state Hargovinddas Kantawala to Gandhi. By 1919 Gandhi was not an unknown or somewhat odd visitor from South Africa. He had established the Ashram at Ahmedabad, launched the *satyagraha* at Champaran and at Kheda, fasted in the cause of the mill-hands of Ahmedabad and launched two journals: *Navajivan* and *Young India.*

It is safe to assume that in 1919 (as in 2019) most Gujarati writers would not have read the *Hind Swaraj*, even as a banned book (and even less likely in Gandhi's own English translation of it). If they had they would have been wonderstruck by Gandhi's Gujarati prose and his ability to be a bilingual thinker; that is not only to think in two languages but also think about two civilisational conditions in two languages simultaneously. The bilingualism that I wish to suggest indicates simultaneity, it suggests a process where an idea is conceived and thought in one language and expressed in another, where it becomes possible to speak of a concept, a notion, alien to one linguistic/semantic universe through another tongue.

Hind Swaraj (or *Hind Swarajya* as originally titled) was written in Gujarati.[1] The only major work that Gandhi himself chose to translate into English. Let us first consider the curious case of the title itself. Gandhi's handwritten manuscript as also the first *Indian Opinion* edition consistently used the term *Rajya*; it is *Hind Swarajya* and not *Hind Swaraj*. The term *Rajya* is used in the text as well; for example, chapter 4 is *Swarajya te shu?* And not *Swaraj te shu?* But during the English translation done soon after and published on 20 March 1910, the term *Rajya* was substituted by *Raj*; and this usage was standardised in subsequent Gujarati editions; beginning with the 1914 edition.

The reason for this change becomes clear if we examine the English rendering. The English rendering was published under the title *Indian Home Rule*.[2] The term *Swarajya/Swaraj* was rendered as *Home Rule* in the English edition in the initial chapters. For example in chapter 1 the term *Swarajya/Swaraj* occurs twenty times. In every instance save one, the term has been rendered as Home Rule. Once it has been rendered as self-government while in one instance, it has been rendered as 'Home- or self-rule.' A semantic shift is introduced in chapter 4, where all seven usages of the term *Swarajya/Swaraj* have been rendered as *Swaraj* in the English edition. This shift became necessary, as Gandhi wanted to introduce a basic semantic difference between the term Home Rule and Swaraj as conceived by him. The term Home Rule had both a pre-history and an identifiable political organisation and persons who aspired after Home Rule. *Swaraj* as Gandhi thought of it was constituted by a different philosophical ground. This difference was clearly articulated by Gandhi in chapter 14. He says that hitherto the reader and the editor had been considering the conditions of freeing India 'indirectly', but would now do so 'directly.' The term directly is an inadequate rendering of the Gujarati term *swa-rupe*, in its 'intrinsic form.' The difference between Home Rule and *Swaraj* for Gandhi is of this intrinsic form. Therefore, Gandhi needed two terms Home Rule and *Swaraj* to speak of the basic differences between two visions and two methods of obtaining them.

The term *Swaraj* occurs fifty-six times in the Gujarati text. The English rendering alternates between Home Rule and Swaraj, the choice being guided by the context of usage and the distance or proximity that he wished to suggest with his own vision.[3] He even qualified the usage by introducing terms such as 'true nature' and 'our goal' to mark the distance.

This distance between Home Rule and *Swaraj* is latent in the Gujarati version. Gandhi did not distinguish between Home Rule and Swaraj in such a shared sense, where he continued to use *Swaraj* to mean both home rule and *Swaraj* in its 'intrinsic form.' But the difference was present before him even while he wrote the Gujarati *Hind Swaraj*. The change from *Rajya* to *Raj* is indicative of that. The term *Rajya*, both in Sanskrit and in Gujarati has a sense of territoriality. *Rajya* is rendered as kingdom, country, or realm. *Raj* on the other hand suggests 'to reign,' 'to rule over.' The idea of reigning in the sense to 'rule ourselves' is basic to Gandhi's idea of *Swaraj*. 'It is Swaraj when we learn to rule ourselves.' The change from *Rajya* to *Raj* was necessary. In Gujarati, he needed to distinguish between two notions of rule, one that denoted territoriality and the other, which suggested rule over oneself. The term *Rajya* did not allow the second and more primary sense to be foregrounded. The nature of this imperative becomes clear when we read the two texts together where the idea of self-rule, self-control and possibility of knowing oneself are clearly marked. It is for this reason that he rendered *Swaraj* as 'rule himself.'

The Gujarati text has retained the term *Swarajya* in two instances, both in chapter twenty. In both instances, it occurs with its opposite *Para Rajya*, foreign rule and *Swarajya* has been rendered as Home Rule in English.

There is another possibility, however speculative, which should be mentioned. The term *Hindvi Swarajya* is closely identified with the writings of V. D. Savarkar. *Hind Swarajya* was far too close for comfort to Savarkar's notion of a *Hindu Pad Padshahi. Hind Swaraj* allowed Gandhi to distance himself even more from Savarkar's vision and his usage.[4]

Far more instructive is the notion that forms the core of *Hind Swaraj*, the idea of *Sudhar. Sudhar* in Gujarati has a lineage. Before Gandhi, the term *sudhar* was used largely to indicate the idea and process of social and religious reform. The term *Sudhar* in the sense of reform did include the idea that *su-dhar* was the good path, the righteous path. And it is in the sense of *su-dhar* being the good path that *sudharo* could be equated with 'good conduct.' But in the history of the term *sudharo* was not indicative of 'that mode of conduct that points out to man the path of duty,' where 'performance of duty and observance of morality' become 'convertible terms,' which allow us to 'attain mastery over our mind and passion' and 'so doing, we know ourselves.' *Sudharo* that makes possible self-knowledge and self-rule are unique to Gandhi. Even after one century of the publication of *Hind Swaraj* the term *sudharo* is used in Gujarati primarily in the nineteenth century sense of reform.

Let us examine this usage more closely. The term *sudhar/sudharo* occurs ninety-six times in the Gujarati text, in fact more than either the term *vachak* (reader) or *adhipati* (editor). It is only when we read the text bilingually that we begin to understand the multiple meanings that Gandhi imbued the term with. In the English rendering *sudhar/sudharo* has been conceived as civilisation, modern civilisation, European civilisation, ancient civilisation, Indian civilisation, reform, progress, and even ephemeral civilisation. The term thus has been conceived and rendered in eight distinct senses. It is clear that Gandhi thought through these distinct terms in English and rendered them into Gujarati through the generic usage *sudharo*. The choice of the term *sudharo* is somewhat perplexing. Gandhi at the time of writing *Hind Swaraj* was aware of the nineteenth-century reform movement in Gujarat and Gujarati. He had read the works of Narmad, Manibhai Nabhubhai and Govardhanram Tripathi.[5] He had read Mahipatram Rupram Mehta and Karsandas Mulji's accounts of the English life. He was aware of the contributions of Parsi reformers like Beharamji Malabari. Gandhi of 1909 did not hold either the reformist practices or the lives of the reformers in good esteem; one suspects that it was the lives of the reformers that perturbed him more than their writings; although his first response when Harilal left home was, 'This is the outcome of reading *Sarasvatichandra*.' He was of course referring to Govardhanram Tripathi's canonical four-part novel where its graduate hero, deeply disappointed with his father leaves home on a journey of self-discovery.

Gandhi had a choice of two other and more prevalent usages to indicate civilisation. These are *sabhyata* and *sanskriti*.

In fact, when Gandhi writes in the English rendering that 'the Gujarati equivalent for civilisation means "good conduct"' he is referring to *sabhyata* rather than *sudharo*. The Gujarati lexicon *BhagvadGoMandal* in fact says that the equivalent of *sanskriti* means civilisation. Gandhi may not have preferred a notion of civilisation that is intrinsically tied to Sanskrit and all the modes of thought and practices that were articulated through that language. But this still does not explain the choice of the term *sudhar*.

Gandhi was clearly invoking *sudhar* in two senses, which have been latent in Gujarati. *Su-dhar* not just as good path, but one that holds, bears, from the Sanskrit root *dhri, dharayati*. One, which holds and bears human society, is *sudhar* and only such *sudhar* could point out to man the path of duty and open the possibility of self-knowledge. *Sudhar* is civilisation in this sense. Secondly, *sudhar* unlike the two other terms has a sense of movement. *Sudhar* according to *BhagvadGoMandal* suggests a movement towards virtue. It entails a choice in favour of the good and active shunning of all that is undesirable. It is this active, choice-enabling, virtue-enhancing possibility of *sudhar* that Gandhi desired from civilisation.

Moreover, *sudhar* in the more prevalent usage could also suggest reform, progress, contemporariness, change and influence of the modern West, all the other senses which are present in the English rendering.

There are instances in the Gujarati text where Gandhi has qualified the term *sudharo*. The term modern civilisation of the English text occurs in three distinct ways in the Gujarati text: as *sudharo*, as *aaj-kal no sudharo* and as *adhunik sudharo*. The term *aaj-kal* in Gujarati literally means today and tomorrow. It is used to indicate contemporary and therefore transient nature of things; the term 'modern' lacks this pronounced sense of transience. Interestingly, the term *adhunik* which occurs only twice in the Gujarati text also has a sense of transience, of lack of permanence in Gujarati. Narmad in his *Narma-Kosha* explained *adhunika*, that which is of present moment as *na take tevu* (that which will not last, ephemeral).[6] By describing civilisation as *adhunik Sudharo* Gandhi wished to emphasise not so much its modernity but the transient nature of what passes under the name civilisation. Therefore Gandhi declared that 'This civilisation is such that one has only to be patient and it will be self-destroyed.' In the Gujarati text he emphasised the self-destructive nature of modern civilisation by stating that *Te sudharo nashkarak ane nashvant che.* (This civilisation is destructive and certain to be destroyed.) This added emphasis is absent in the English text. In contemporary Gujarati both *sudharo* as civilisation and *adhunik* as ephemeral have become recessive, we speak of *adhunik* in the sense of *navin* and hence modern.

In the Gujarati text, the term *kudhar/kudharo* (the wrong path) creates a play between *sudhar* and *kudhar*. The term occurs nine times in the Gujarati text, which has been rendered in English as 'civilisation only in name,' 'civilisation as a disease' and 'reverse of civilisation.' In fact, six out of nine times Gandhi did not render the term *kudhar* in the English text. This is true of many of the idiomatic Gujarati phrases. Gandhi either does not render them in English, or chooses to provide a literal translation. He does not resort to equivalent idiomatic usages in English. For example, the Gujarati idiom *Miya ne Mahadev ne na bane* (Miya and Mahadev will always quarrel) is used to frame the argument about Hindu–Muslim relations and the *had ver* (inborn enmity) between the two communities. This idiom is used twice in the Gujarati text. Gandhi chose not to render it in English at all. Once he rendered it as 'Our very proverbs prove it,' and in the second instance as 'The proverbs you have quoted' while in case of *Jenu man changa che tene gher bethe ganga che*, Gandhi provided a literal translation: 'those whose hearts were aglow with righteousness have the Ganges in their own home.'

Gandhi does something similar with the English phrases that occur in the Gujarati text. In most instances they appear in their English usage, but in some crucial cases, Gandhi used the native, vernacular expressions of English terms, like *korato* (for courts) or *dactaro* (for doctors). This practice was not without intent. Gandhi used these vernacular expressions to distinguish between those institutions and practices, which were rooted in Indian civilisation from those, which came as part of the modern West. For instance in the Gujarati text he consistently used the terms *tabib, hakim* and *vaidya* to distinguish Indian healing systems and practitioners from *dactaro* who were trained in modern European medicine. This difference is obliterated in the English text, except in two cases; once he employed the term *vaidya* in the English text and once he used the expression 'honest physician' to describe English doctors who did not encourage a free play of passions. Similarly, the Gujarati text employs both *adalat* and *korato*; the former denoting the Indian justice delivery system and the later where barristers practised.

There is a Gujarati expression which owes it resonance to Gandhi's self-practice of spinning. This expression is *jhinu kantvu,* to spin a fine yarn. It indicates also to the capacity to pay attention to minute details, to care for details that seem insignificant. In present day Gujarat (and I suspect even in Gandhi's time) it was not always used in a positive sense; it is quite often seen as an unnecessary practice deployed to confuse rather than clarify. It is futile labour. The Gujarati litterateurs are known for their disdain for such *jhinu kantvu.*

The foregoing reading of *Hind Swaraj* in the prevalent Gujarati usage is an example of *jhinu kantvu,* not entirely necessary or useful.

But despite such lack of attention to Gandhi's prose or his mode of thought today (or more appropriately several decades ago) the Parishad seemed somewhat, just somewhat, embarrassed by its choice. One way to deal with embarrassment is forgetting; Milan Kundera would say laughter and forgetting. We, Gujaratis, as a culture are not very comfortable at laughing at ourselves. And for that reason we forget. As in Kundera's novel *The Book of Laughter and Forgetting*, the Gujarati Sahitya Parishad decided to air-brush this event from our history (our pragmatism helps in forgetting, but that would be belabouring another cultural trait). Three of the most eminent scholars—and among them certified Gandhians as well—Uma Shankar Joshi, Anant Rai Raval and the deputy editor of Gandhi's collected works, C. N. Patel, decided to make this matter disappear.

Gandhi accepted to be the president of the Parishad not to avenge the defeat. He did so, because he had a clear perspective on the role and place of literature in the national life and not just the life of the nation. To Gandhi at least it was clear that the unease that the literary classes of Gujarat felt about his prose and his reading of literature had not entirely disappeared, this despite the fact that some years before this meeting Gandhi had published his autobiography, *Satya Na Prayogo*, and there was nothing unrefined or crude about the language of the autobiography.

Munshi announced to the conference that Gandhi had 'resolutely' taken up the responsibility, and added for good measure that Gandhi's resolute acceptance was as firm as his decision to decline in 1925.

Gandhi in his opening remarks clarified this and stated his lack of enthusiasm for the honour. 'When friends from whom I expect to take some work put some burden on me, I persuade myself to assume it.'[7] The significance of the twelfth meeting was not lost on Gandhi. The twelfth day rites are the most important of death rituals. Those who expected him to perform the *sharaddha* of the Parishad were disappointed when he said, not entirely in jest 'but I am afraid, I won't be performing the twelfth day rites of the conference! That inauspicious wordhas fallen to my lot.'[8] Before he moved to the literary matters he chose to address the character and the constitution of the literary body. There were demands to make the institution more democratic, which was tantamount to freeing the institution from Munshi's control. Gandhi did not agree that constitutions of institutions could or should be changed to address particular instance or person. Nor did he believe that without literature itself changing its orientation the Parishad could have a meaningful contribution to make to the national life. What was required, Gandhi believed, was to free the world of literature, make it autonomous from the wealthy merchant class.

In 1933 he had donated 10,000 books from the Ashram and Vidyapith library, which included a substantial collection of his personal books to start the first major public library—the Maneklal Jethalal Library—of Ahmedabad.[9] At the time of its dedication Gandhi had expressed his desire to have in Ahmedabad the best library and public institution that could draw people to it. He cautioned that libraries are not created or nurtured by merchants. 'Do not have as your librarian a merchant who can only preserve your books but also have someone who appreciates them and can select them. Do not think of having a worldly-wise on your committee, only the learned will know what a good library is, and how it can shine forth.'[10]

Gandhi had created the first major centres of Indology, religious studies and archaeology at Gujarat Vidyapith and knew the significance of the archive. Knowledge in the hands of the wealthy, Gandhi argued, could only lead to decline in knowledge; it could also lead to the decline in Dharma itself. 'In Gujarat a priceless collection of books lies in the custody of the merchant class. Beautiful collections of Jain literature are wrapped up in their silk clothes. My heart is sore at the sight of these books. What use can these books be when they have fallen in the hands of ignorant merchants who can only pile up wealth? The Jain religion, too, is withering in their hands because they have reduced Dharma to formal business. Indeed can Dharma adjust itself to the ways of commerce? It is for commerce to adjust itself to claims of Dharma.'[11]

The wealthy class had also gathered at the Sahitya Parishad on 31 October 1936, in what was to be Gandhi's last visit to the city. In his welcome address Sir Chinubhai had questioned Gandhi's fitness to preside over the Parishad. He had said that Gandhi was neither a scholar nor a literary figure. And in an apparent and pre-meditated insult he had referred to Gandhi's Vidyapith—Gandhi had on the previous day presided over its convocation as its Chancellor—in the past tense.

Gandhi in his address dealt with both the charges. He asserted his *adhikar*—his fitness—to preside over the Parishad. 'However, I am the *Kulpati* of Vidyapith; I was instrumental in having the *Jodani Kosh* prepared.'[12] On Vidyapith he was more forceful. 'I shall beg leave to inform him that the Vidyapith still exists and will continue to exist. It is not a passing phase. The Vidyapith will continue to function so long as we do not forget the mantra of *Swaraj*.'[13] The Vidyapith, he reminded Sir

Chinubhai and the gentry of Ahmedabad, had been created to build up the country and not a 'depot' where parents could leave their painted dolls to be returned untouched after a period of time. 'The Vidyapith is not meant for the painted dolls and dandies of Ahmedabad. Bhai Ambalal's daughter may have joined it. But the Vidyapith is not a "depot" to which dolls would come to be decorated only to be "delivered" to their parents just as they had come, i.e., return to their care. The Vidyapith has been formed to build up country men and country women.'[14]

Having dealt with the doubts that the Gujarati middle-class and merchant-capitalists harboured about him and continued to do, Gandhi moved on to ask the basic question that he wanted to pose, the reason for which he had accepted to preside over the conference. 'For whose sake are we going to have our literature?'[15] 'Not certainly for the great gentry of Ahmedabad. They can engage great literary men and have libraries in their homes.'[16] He recalled his neighbour in Kocharab Ashram, a man who worked his bullocks with abuse to goad them to pull water from a well. Gandhi said that he had asked the poet Narasinharao Divetia for some inspired tunes and ditties that the man could lustily sing and forget his abuse. Gandhi said that it was given to an extraordinary poet, not a novelist, to approach him. 'What can I say to him? Anyone who is a poet should approach him. Munshi is a novelist, he cannot do so. Only an extraordinary artist can go and persuade him. A couple of words here and a couple of words there and he would be put the thing in a way that he will be able to catch the meaning.'[17]

Gandhi said that he was the self-appointed representative of the illiterate and voiceless India. How was he to give them life-giving literature? He had set up a library in the village

Segaon, but what was the library to contain? 'What am I to read them? Munshi's novels? Or *Krishnacharitra* that Sjt Krishnalal Jhaveri has translated from Bengali? It is a good book but I am afraid I cannot place it before these illiterate folks.'[18] What he needed was poetry.

Gandhi's Gujarati writings are suffused with poetry, one form of literature that he was drawn to and knew intimately was poetry. He was a discerning reader of poetry, the anthology of Bhakti poetry that he helped create through his practice of recitation—the *Ashram Bhajanavali*—remains one of the finest anthologies of its kind.

He was also an accomplished translator of verse, albeit in prose form. Tulsidas and Surdas, Mira and Narsinh Mehta, Shamal Bhatt, Akho, Dhiro Bhagat were like the Bhagavat Gita and Isa Upanishad 'by-hearted' by him. Their verses, quite often just a fleeting image from a poem, found their way in his writing. Gandhi's autobiography in Gujarati, and in a very different way in English, is immersed in poetry. At least four titles of his chapters are poetic verse. In fact, the only title to appear untranslated in English is Surdas' *Nirbal Ke Bal Rama*. The poetic sensibility also informs the English translation. For instance in the chapter *Nirbal Ke Bal Rama* the combined sensibility of Gandhi and his translator Mahadev Desai are on display. Sets of prosaic sentences of Gujarati soar in the English translation with the help of verses. The Gujarati states *banne haath hetha pade* (when all actions become futile); it is translated through Henry Francis Lyte's hymn 'Abide with Me' with the lines 'when helpers fail and comforts flee'. A few lines later the phrase *hriday ni nirmalta* (purity of heart) is rendered as 'emptied of all but love' from Charles Wesley's hymn. Soon thereafter Gandhi writes of *gagan gami sur* (music reaching to the heavens) which is rendered through a line from

Alfred Tennyson's line from 'Locksley Hall', 'trembling pass in music out of sight.'

In his address Gandhi spoke of a book that he called a treasure of English language. The book that he invoked was Dean Farrar's *Life of Christ*. This is not a work of poetry, it is not verse. In fact it is a large prose work of over four hundred pages. And yet, Gandhi felt that this was a work of poetry and a book that he could place in the hands of his peasant neighbours in Segaon. He asked, 'Have we men like Farrar who will produce great literature for village folk? Our literary men will pore over Kalidasa and Bhavabhuti, and English authors, and will give us imitations.'[19] Villagers, he asserted had no use for such persons.

What then is poetry for Gandhi or more pertinently who is a poet? Poetry, Gandhi says is written in 'faith and prayer'; any work that is so imbued is poetry and its writer a poet. Faith for Gandhi has two aspects; faith in the essential goodness of all human beings; not that he does not have a notion of evil, but without the faith in the potential of all human beings to recognise pain and suffering of others and act on it Satyagraha could not be. It is for this reason that that *Vaishnava Jana To* was one of his favourite poems. The other aspect of faith is the belief in the ultimate measure of Truth, truth that Is, truth that alone can be the only true measure of order of things.

Prayer is an act of waiting; waiting upon God as Truth to illuminate the inner-life, an act of preparation, of cleansing, of *upvas*, of being closer to Him so that one can acquire the capacity to glimpse at the truth that lies covered by a golden orb.

Literature to be life-giving had to be imbued with faith and prayer; only such art, Gandhi said, could provide an unmediated experience; only such art could have the power to capture the uninitiated. That very morning Gandhi had been taken to an art exhibition. The art works of Ravishankar Raval, Gujarat's foremost painter, celebrated as Kala Guru, were on display. But Gandhi had come away disappointed. 'I missed what I would call painting that speaks. Why should I need the artist to explain the work of art to me?'[20] He recalled being captivated by a statue of Christ on a cross in Vatican, that simply captured him and held him spell-bound, that was still before him, and a statuette in Belur near Mysore from a broken bracket of an ancient temple that 'spoke out to me without anyone to help me understand it.'[21] Gandhi said that he wanted art and literature that would speak to the millions. He displayed rare emotion in conclusion. 'My heart is weeping at the present moment, but time has made it hard enough not to break even when there are occasions for it. As I think of Segaon and its skeletons [at this point he broke down and wept] as I think of Segaon and its folks I can't help saying that our literature is a miserable affair.'[22]

He addressed the Parishad two days later, on 2nd November. That was to be his last day in Ahmedabad. He never returned to the town in which he had built his Ashram and his Vidyapith, for the rest of his life. In his concluding speech he lamented that novels had widowed the Gujarati language. Novel that he referred to is both a literary form and a state of mind. 'Today we have a spate of novels. Reading novels has become a passion. These are sprouting, like mushrooms. If you want to know how a novel is written I can tell you a good deal about it. But it cannot be described before civilized men and women. One's imagination runs riot, it knows no restraint.'[23]

Imagination that runs riot and knows no restraint is the opposite of the state of *sthitapragna*, a state where the intellect is secure, a state that Gandhi aspired to. Novels by exciting the imagination lead one to forget oneself. Therefore Gandhi said: 'We can do without these novels. The Gujarati language will not be widowed without them. At present it is indeed in the state of widowhood.'[24]

The poverty of Gujarati language, Gandhi argued cannot be wiped by an increase in novels. Gandhi's denial of the novel is not entirely on the aesthetic ground, it is also not wholly based on the subject matter of Gujarati novels. Poetry as we recall is an act of faith and prayer, even a work of prose so imbued is a poem for Gandhi. Why is it that a novel cannot be a work of faith and prayer?

Novel is called *naval katha* in Gujarati, literally, a new story. The modern, the *naval*, the *adhunik* for Gandhi is the cause of India's slavery. India for him was being ground down not under the British heel but under the weight of the modern civilisation. This modernity for Gandhi precluded the possibility of moral conduct, it restricted civilisational possibility of self-knowledge. Modern civilisation with its outward orientation and its desire to increase bodily comforts changed the very ground from which questions of human worth are posed. It is a state where machines are the measure of men. In such a civilisation neither self-knowledge, which is essential for *moksha*, for moral action and *Swaraj* are possible. The state of unrestrained imagination running riot is the state opposite of *brahmacharya*, not as celibacy but as a state of equipoise where all senses are in harmony with one another, wherein the pursuit of truth and conduct of truth are possible. The novel being an artefact of the modern world has predilection for the body, specifically the female body. In what is the first statement on the prevalence of the description of the female body in Gujarati, Gandhi warned against such distortions. '... Whether God has created them in order that men would describe their bodies? There was no reason to believe that they were created to cook and clean utensils.'[25] Why are women not described as they really are, Gandhi asked. 'They are neither Rambhas, celestial maidens, nor slave girls. They too are independent human beings.'[26] Such wrong apotheosis of women permeated the current Gujarati writings. Gandhi said, 'She poor soul feels that she is not as she is described, how can she become so?'[27]

Gandhi in fact, wished to introduce a resolution about the nature and purpose of writing, but remained content with only a suggestion. 'I entreat our writers to begin writing for our dumb masses rather than our city-dwellers.'[28]

In February of 1916, Gandhi was obliged to speak at the Kashi Nagari Pracharini Sabha. He began by making an apology. 'I feel ashamed that before you I cannot speak well in Hindi. You know that I used to live in South Africa. It was there that I learnt a little Hindi while working with my Indian brethren. You will therefore forgive me my failing.'[29] This was no customary apology. Hindi was a language that he had not formally learnt.

Sudhir Chandra, comparing and commenting upon Gandhi's facility with the three languages that he spoke and wrote in, observed: 'Properly schooled in both, Gandhi was perfectly at home with Gujarati and English. For all his minimalism, there was about his Gujarati and English an unmistakably Gandhian grace and elegance. His, in these two languages, was the minimalism of one who, possessing a wealth of words, allusions and associations, had chosen to make less more. But in Hindi, a language he never formally learnt, his minimalism was of one who possessed just about what he needed. Without fail, in contradistinction to the polish and elegance of his Gujarati and English, his Hindi was quaint, odd and awkward.'[30]

In that meeting Gandhi made a statement that he chose not to elaborate. 'Freedom cannot be gained without literature.'[31] The word that he had used for freedom in Hindi was *Swatantrata*. It was for Gandhi the function of literature to bring to people higher thoughts and new ideas. The capacity of the mind to imagine the state of freedom is the gift of literature that Gandhi wished to cherish.

Two years later, in 1918, Gandhi was invited to preside over the Hindi Sahitya Sammelan at Indore. In his presidential address he spoke of the relationship between knowledge, the dynamic energy of the people and the spirt of a language.

Seventeen years later he was called back to preside over the Sammelan, which was to take place in Indore. While advocating the need for Hindi to see itself as a national language Gandhi spoke of the need for Hindi to acquire universality through absorption of words from other languages. 'Every living language has this capacity to absorb words from other languages. That is how it acquires universality. What has English not adopted? There are so many Latin and Greek idioms that have been absorbed into English. They have not spared even modern languages. Their impartiality in this is praiseworthy. English has borrowed many Hindustani words. Some words taken from African languages are also found in English. In this the English have maintained their policy of 'free trade'. In saying this I do not mean that we should indiscriminately introduce words from other languages into Hindi as English-educated youths of today do. This should be done with discretion. We are not paupers, but we shall not also be miserly. We shall call a chair a '*kursi*' not '*chatushpadapith*".'[32]

But strangely Gandhi was not entirely open to the same diversity of expression in Gujarati. A few years before the 1936 Sahitya Parishad, K. M. Munshi had asked Gandhi to write a foreword to his *Gujarat and Its Literature.* Gandhi wrote, 'The survey naturally confines itself to the language understood and spoken by the middle class. Commercially-minded and self-satisfied, their language has naturally been "effeminate and sensuous". Of the language of the people we know next to nothing. We hardly understand their speech. The gulf between them and us, the middle class, is so great that we do not know them and they know still less of what we think and speak.'[33]

The contribution of Parsis and Muslims to modern Gujarati came in for a special mention. 'Munshi has alluded to Parsi-Gujarati. So there is. It is unfortunate that there is Parsi-Gujarati. It is confined to novels and stories of the shilling-shocker style. They are meant merely for passing the idle hour. The language is tortured out of shape. And just as there is Parsi-Gujarati there is also Muslim-Gujarati though on a much humbler scale. It is impossible to ignore these two streams. They are not wells of Gujarati undefiled. But no reviewer of Gujarati literature can afford to ignore the existence of works which hundreds, if not thousands, of Parsis and Muslims read and by which, maybe, even shape part of their conduct.'[34]

Gandhi had begun to reflect on the Parsi Gujarati and the special responsibility of the Parsis to their mother-tongue as early as 1909. Speaking at a Gujarati meeting in London on 5 October 1909 Gandhi expressed hope that Gujarati—which had come to be derided as merely the language of commerce—would be served by three great religions, Hinduism, Islam and

Zoroastrianism. 'The same thought can sometimes be expressed in Gujarati in three different ways. The Gujarati that a Muslim writes will reflect the traces of Arabic and the Persian of Sheikh Sanda; the Parsi-Gujarati will reveal the influence of Zoroastra's Zend and Gujarati of a Hindu that of Sanskrit.'[35]

Gandhi was conscious of the plural character of the Gujarati language. He had very different expectations from the Parsis. Hindus and Muslims of India speak all Indian languages, while 'Parsis, so to say, were sent by *Khuda* from Iran exclusively for the service of Gujarati.'[36] The Parsis owned newspapers and printing presses in Gujarati and for that reason could exercise great influence over the language and its progress. But their Gujarati according to Gandhi left a great deal to be desired. He had only one request to make to them. 'Please do not murder what has now become your mother-tongue and which you can never give up.'[37] Gandhi said that it was a matter of great regret that Parsis were determined to spite the language in respect of pronunciation and spelling.

Thus, while acknowledging the desirability of multiple forms of Gujarati, the wide gulf between the effete and sensuous language of the middle class and the tongue of the people, Gandhi is advocating a certain standard—a kind of pure Gujarati. Gandhi gave examples of Parsi poets like Behramji Malabari and Ardeshar Khabardar who had enriched Gujarati. The Parsi argument that their Gujarati should be accepted as genuine Gujarati does not meet with Gandhi's approval. 'That Gujarati which is spoken and written by hundreds of thousands of educated people who have their home in Gujarat is true Gujarati … In what sort of Gujarati shall we frame our laws? In what sort of Gujarati shall we write our text-books?'[38]

Paradoxically, by Gandhi's own logic, the Gujarati that the middle-class Hindu Gujarati spoke became the measure of the purity of the Gujarati tongue. Gandhi went a step ahead, he linked the love of language with the love for the country. Gandhi found that a community that was as patriotic, had as much love for the country as the Parsis, would show no eagerness to cultivate the love of the language.

Gandhi, while admitting different styles of speech and different vocabularies, wanted uniform rules of writing. To save Gujarati orthography from disfigurement Gandhi got the Gujarat Vidyapith to impose order on Gujarati *jodni*. In 1928 Gandhi declared that the Vidyapith, under the leadership of Kakasaheb Kalelkar—a native speaker of Marathi—'is preparing a dictionary such as never been attempted in Gujarati language.'[39] Gandhi had hoped that this *Jodni Kosha* would end the complete laxity with regard to spelling that plagued Gujarati. A language without fixed spelling, Gandhi said, was akin to a man without nose. 'A language which does not possess a universally accepted dictionary but admits all words in it may be regarded as ownerless. We have inexhaustible means at our disposal for checking spellings of English words … Gujarati is the only language that has hitherto remained ownerless.'[40] With the publication of the *Jodni Kosha* in April 1929, Gujarati acquired its first orthographic dictionary. The dictionary printed in 373 pages had 43,743 words and was sold at the cost of three rupees, with the Vidyapith providing a subsidy. When the first 500 copies came out Gandhi declared that henceforth Gujarati spellings should be written as given in the dictionary. He wrote in the foreword—which is carried till this day—'After the publication of this dictionary now no one has the right to do as his fancy dictates in the matter of spellings.'[41]

How was one to accept that the spellings given in the Vidyapith *Jodni Kosha* were correct? This was not of paramount concern to Gandhi. 'The answer is that it is not a question of deciding which spellings are correct and which are not. The principle followed in the compilation of this dictionary is that the spellings adopted by those who have good knowledge of Gujarati and who try to write grammatically correct Gujarati be accepted as correct.'[42]

The second edition was published soon after the publication of the first edition; Gandhi and Vidyapith's ambition went a step further. Not content with fixing spellings, the second edition of the *Saarth Jodni Kosha* provided in brief current meanings of the words.

Gandhi's quest for simplicity and purity led him to an endeavour to fix the cognitive universe of the Gujaratis.

Notes

1. *Hind Swarajya* was written in Gujarati between 13 and 22 November 1909 on board *Kildonan Castle* and was published in two installments in the Gujarati section of *Indian Opinion* (11 and 19 December 1909). The original handwritten manuscript runs into 276 pages (275+5 pages of introduction). It has 88 questions posed by *Vachak Varg* (a group of readers, literally) and 88 responses by the editor. The entire manuscript has 228 marks of erasure or correction, of which 21 belong to the section of the reader while the remaining 207 to the part of the editor. This may have been for two reasons: one of length and the other of clarity. It is tempting to think that Gandhi had more clarity regarding the questions and showed more tentativeness in his formulations in the editor's voice.
2. The title of the English edition was changed to *Hind Swaraj or Indian Home Rule* in 1921, all subsequent editions of the English text appear under this combined title, except the 1924 American edition edited by Haridas T. Majumdar which was titled *Sermon on the Sea.*

3. Out of 56 occurrences of the term *Swaraj* in Gujarati it has been rendered as *Home Rule* in 28 instances.
4. I am grateful to Ganesh Devy for this.
5. The identification of reformers with the act of writing is very strong in Gandhi. In fact he rendered *Paschim Na Sudharako* (Western Reformers) as Western Writers.
6. The first part of *Narma-Kosha* was published in November 1861, the second in December 1862, the third in September 1864 and the fourth part in August 1866. The complete *Narma-Kosha* was published in 1873. The term *adhunik* is described on page 58.
7. *CWMG*, vol. 63, p. 408.
8. *Ibid.*
9. Of these merely 3822 books survive. These are available in digital format on the Gandhi Heritage Portal.
10. *CWMG*, vol. 56, pp. 16–17.
11. *Ibid,* p. 17.
12. *CWMG,* vol. 63, p. 412.
13. *Ibid.*
14. *Ibid.*
15. *Ibid.*
16. *Ibid.*
17. *Ibid.*
18. *Ibid,* p. 415.
19. *Ibid.*
20. *Ibid,* p. 416.
21. *Ibid.*
22. *Ibid.*
23. *Ibid,* p. 419.
24. *Ibid.*
25. *Ibid.* p. 421.
26. *Ibid*
27. *Ibid.*
28. *Ibid.* p. 420.
29. *CWMG,* vol. 13, p. 209.
30. Sudhir Chandra, "Gandhi's Hindi and His Aesthetics of Poverty", Unpublished essay.
31. *CWMG,* vol. 13, p. 209.

32. *CWMG*, vol. 60, p. 449.
33. *CWMG,* vol. 61, p. 26.
34. *Ibid.* p. 27.
35. *CWMG,* vol. 9, pp. 459–460.
36. *Ibid.* p. 460.
37. *Ibid.*
38. *CWMG*, vol. 19, pp. 507–508.
39. *CWMG*, vol. 37, p. 281.
40. *CWMG,* vol. 35, p. 204
41. *CWMG,* vol. 40, p. 213.
42. *Ibid.*

References

1. Sharma, Suresh and Tridip Suhrud (ed.). 2009, reprinted 2019. *M K Gandhi's Hind Swaraj: A Critical Edition.* New Delhi: Orient BlackSwan.
2. Dave, Narmadashankar Lalshankar. 1861, 1862, 1863, 1873. *Narma Kosha*. Published in four parts from Mumbai by the author.
3. Kundera, Milan. 1996. Transl. from the French by Aaron Asher. *The Book of Laughter and Forgetting.* London: Faber & Faber.
4. Munshi, K M. 1935, reprinted 1954. *Gujarat and Its Literature.* Mumbai: Bharatiya Vidya Bhavan.
5. *The Collected Works of Mahatma Gandhi.* New Delhi: Publications Division.

Reading Gandhi in Two Tongues

Gandhi records the deep embarrassment with which he admitted to his Theosophist friends in London that he had read the *Gita* neither in Sanskrit nor in Gujarati. He said: 'They talked to me about the Gita. They were reading Sir Edwin Arnold's translation – *The Song Celestial* – and they invited me to read the original with them. I felt ashamed, as I had read the divine poem neither in Sanskrit nor in Gujarati.'[1] He read the Gita first in translation and only then in Sanskrit and Gujarati. His acquaintance with the life of Buddha was also through Sir Edwin's biographical poem, *The Light of Asia*.

This experience was not unusual. He was reflecting on what was a common experience of many young men of India in the later half of the nineteenth century. Acquaintance with one's own culture, with tradition, history, and religion through the medium of English language and Western education was a common feature of colonial cultural exchange. It was as if one defined oneself through the English eyes and in the English language. However, we are not concerned here with the impact of colonialism on Gandhi or his responses to it. Our primary concern is with the act of translation. In this, we shall have to deal with Gandhi's reading of Western Civilization.

Gandhi was a serious student of languages. He believed that as a leader he ought to communicate with the people in their own languages. Gandhi read and wrote three languages with a certain degree of ease. Gujarati, his mother tongue,

---

This essay first appeared in *Reading Gandhi and Other Essays* published by the Indian Institute of Advanced Study, 2012. Used by permission.

English and Hindustani, which he hoped would become the national language of India. His lifelong quest was to be able to communicate with the people of India in their own tongues and in their own idioms. He therefore made serious attempts to learn various Indian languages. When he was in South Africa, he tried to learn Tamil and Telugu, two languages from South India. In fact, he published his weekly newspaper *Indian Opinion* in Gujarati and English and it often carried certain pages in Tamil and Urdu. He learnt Hindi, Urdu, and Bangla. Even on the morning of his assassination, he had his Bangla lessons. He could sign his name in fourteen Indian languages.

We must also remember that Gandhi was a translator. He translated Tolstoy, Ruskin, and Platoís *Defence of Socrates* into Gujarati. He also rendered into English his most important philosophical work *Hind Swaraj*. Gandhi is also one of the most translated writers of Gujarat. He commissioned translations of his books and writings into English. He supervised and authenticated most translations of his work.

After his death, all his writings, speeches, letters, and conversations have been published in 100 volumes of the *Collected Works of Mahatma Gandhi* (CWMG). The *Collected Works of Mahatma Gandhi*[2] are available in three languages, Gujarati, English, and Hindi. Thus, the process of translation of his works went on much after his death and continues even today.

The attempt here will be to understand how Gandhi translated certain key philosophical concepts. This would allow us to understand not only the conceptual categories but also his understanding of the method of translation, its possibilities, and limitations. We will have to use certain Gujarati terms in the process, which I hope to be able to clarify in the closest English equivalent.

Translation fundamentally is a process of communicating meaning across languages, cultures, intellectual traditions, and time. It was no different for Gandhi.

Let us take one example. He was in South Africa when the Transvaal Government proposed changes in the Asiatic Act. The changes made registration of all Asiatics compulsory and demanded that all Asiatics submit impressions of all their fingers, a clause that was seen as humiliating and degrading. Gandhi was a practising Barrister and a very successful one at that. He was trained in Western Law and Jurisprudence; he used English language in courts and in all public discourses in South Africa. It would have been easy for him to understand the implications of the new law in English. His response is fascinating. Describing the process he says: 'I took the Transvaal Government Gazette Extraordinary of August 22, 1906 in which the Ordinance was published, home from the office. I went up a hill near the house in the company of a friend and began to translate the draft Ordinance into Gujarati.'[3] This is remarkable. A Britain trained barrister practising law in South African colony translates a legal ordinance into his mother tongue in order to comprehend the true significance of it! What does this signify? He knew that the Ordinance was intended for the Asiatic community, particularly the Indians. Although drafted in legal language its implications were to be deeply cultural. The cultural significance of this document could be grasped only in the language of the people it was aimed at. The humiliation inherent in that cold, bureaucratic document could be internalised fully only in his own language. It was only after its translation not only in a linguistic sense but also in a cultural sense that any effective opposition to it could be thought of. Thus, for him, translation was a process by which alien notions could be grasped, their meanings internalised, and cultural responses to it could be offered.

Let us take another example of this process. This example deals with the question of the literary form of Autobiography. Autobiography in India is essentially a nineteenth century form. Its emergence was linked with two processes. One was the process of Western education. The second was the movement for social and religious reform that challenged the orthodoxy in the second half of the nineteenth century in various regions of India. Western education brought to young university graduates Western notions of aesthetics, ethics, philosophy, and social organisation. It also introduced them to the practice of writing history in the linear western sense. It brought to them the idea that each person had a unique individual identity. The social and religious reform movement gave them the sense that the old order was changing and a new, modern and more progressive social order was about to emerge. They wanted to capture this process in literary forms. Two very powerful literary forms emerged in the nineteenth century India, the novel and the autobiography. In a culture, which had a long tradition of story telling and story writing, novel as a form, did not pose many cultural problems. It was the autobiography, which was deeply troubling as a literary form. Major Indian philosophical systems had been advocating the self-effacement of individual. It was argued that only by the subjugation of the individual ego that the soul could be sublimated and could eventually be one with the Creator. In such a culture autobiography as a story of the self was seen as introducing major cultural transitions. Therefore, almost all individuals who wrote autobiographies in various Indian languages in the nineteenth century wrote about the difficulty of writing about the self in an alien form. They tried to resolve this tension by claiming that by writing the autobiography in their mother tongue they were modernising the literary tradition of their language.

When Gandhi decided to write his autobiography in 1925, he had to face the same dilemma. How was he to speak about his life in a form that was seen as Western? Would he be endorsing the superiority of Western cultural modes by doing so? He narrates his perplexity: 'But a God-fearing friend had his doubts, which he shared with me on my day of silence. "What has set you on this adventure?" he asked. "Writing an autobiography is a practice peculiar to the West. I know of nobody in the East having written one, except amongst those who have come under Western influence... Don't you think it would be better not to write anything like an autobiography, at any rate just as yet?'[4] Gandhi's unnamed friend is advocating a familiar argument. Autobiography is a form peculiar to the colonisers and those Indians who were colonised. Why should Gandhi the most creative opponent of the colonial culture attempt to write one and in the process endorse a Western practice?

Gandhi's response to this criticism is most creative. He responded: 'This argument had some effect on me. But it is not my purpose to attempt a real autobiography. I simply want to tell the story of my numerous experiments with truth... But I should certainly like to narrate my experiments in the spiritual field which are known only to myself, and from which I have derived such powers as I possess for working in the political field. If the experiments are really spiritual, then there can be no room for self-praise. They can only add to my humility.'[5]

Gandhi is at his creative best in this passage. He distinguishes between what he calls a real autobiography and an autobiography that he would write. A real autobiography is a Western form, a form that can lead to self-praise. But what he wanted to write was not that. His attempt would be to tell a story of his experiments with truth. These experiments were spiritual and moral. A narration of such experiments can only make him and his readers more aware of his limitations and would make him more humble. He takes the Western form of writing about the self and translates it in his own idiom. The Gujarati word for autobiographical writings is *Atmakatha*. The term *Atmakatha* translates as not autobiography but as 'the story of the soul.'

Gandhi here is translating a literary form. We are aware that autobiography in its origins is a Christian practice. In its original sense, it was a story of a soul in search of God. Gandhi by employing autobiography as *Atmakatha* opens up the possibility of speaking of his striving and pinning for self-realization, to see God face to face and to attain *Moksha*. As *Atmakatha* his story of the self would be authentically Indian, as it would speak of his spiritual and moral quest. No one before him or after him in the autobiographical tradition of India would succeed in writing an *Atmakatha*. There is an interesting transposition that happens in the actual act of translating Gandhi's autobiography from Gujarati into English.[6] In the original Gujarati, the main title of the story is *Satya Na Prayogo*, which literally means experiments with truth. The word *Atmakatha* appears as a subtitle. It signifies two things. One, that it is the story of experiments that is primary. Two, it has an autobiographical context as these experiments were done by an individual. The title thus matches with what Gandhi's original intention was. In the English translation, the process is reversed. *An Autobiography* becomes the main title while *Experiments with Truth* is rendered as a subtitle. It indicates not a failure of translation, but a much deeper cultural failure. It indicates the difficulty of speaking about the soul in an alien tongue.

Gandhi is also doing another act of translation in this process. The first act of translation was the transformation of the literary form itself. The second act of translation is that of the method. Gandhi calls it experiments with truth. Let us focus on the word experiments first. Experiment is a method that is deeply associated with Western science. As a method, experiment presupposes two aspects. One is the distance between the subject and the object or between the observer and the observed. Only when this separation between the subject and the object is attained science emerges. This makes science value free and therefore universal. The second is dependent upon the first. An experiment, which is value free and where the distance between the subject and the object is attained leads to truth or a fact that can be verified. Thus, an experiment is a method of arriving at truth. Experiments are not about truth, they lead to what we regard as truth.

Gandhi chooses to call his method experiments; even in Gujarati, he uses the term *Prayogo*, which denotes experimentation. This choice of term is very significant. He had another term available from the spiritual tradition. This term is *Sadhana*. Sadhana is a difficult term to translate into English. It has been variously translated as spiritual practices, as penance and as striving. But Gandhi consciously used the term Prayogo, experiments. He explains why the term Prayogo was chosen over Sadhana in the following way. 'There are some things which are known only to oneself and one's maker. They are clearly incommunicable. The experiments that I am about to relate are not such.'[7] He is saying that if his striving were such that it was communicable only to him and to his God they would be Sadhana. But the experiments that he was referring to were not such. He in fact refers to the scientific method. He says: 'I claim from them nothing more than does a scientist who, though he conducts his experiments with the utmost accuracy, forethought, and minuteness, never claims any finality about his conclusions, but keeps an open mind regarding them. I have gone through deep self-introspection, searched myself through and through, and examined and analysed every psychological situation… For me they appear to be absolutely correct, and seem for the time being to be final.'[8]

Thus, Gandhi applies the Western scientific methods to his spiritual experiments. But he introduces a major transformation in the method. The scientific method necessarily implies division between the subject and the object to arrive at truth. But what Gandhi requires is the scientific method without the separation. So he becomes both the subject and the object in search for truth. Thus, he takes the Western scientific method and turns it into a spiritual practice by destroying the opposition between subject and object.

Gandhi, as a translator, appears to be operating at various levels. He is doing translation to derive meaning, to alter a literary form and even to transform a method of inquiry. Now let us take an example where he seems to be suggesting the non-translatability of an intellectual discipline. The case that we shall take is that of history.

While Gandhi was imprisoned at the Yeravda prison, he decided to write a history. This was to be an account of the Satyagraha in South Africa. He wrote this account in Gujarati while in jail and called it *Dakshin Africa Na Satyagraha No Itihas*. Its exact translation in English would have to be 'A History of Satyagraha in South Africa.' This book was immediately translated into English by his close associate Valji Govindji Desai. This translation was read, verified, and authenticated by Gandhi. The term history itself was omitted from the title of the book. Why? It was clearly not an oversight. It was a deliberate choice. The title of the book in English reads *Satyagraha in South Africa*. To understand the omission of the term history we will have to understand the meaning that he attached to two terms: the Gujarati term *Itihas* and the English term History. Gandhi in fact saw these two as separate. Itihas was not History for him. In his book, the *Hind Swaraj* there is a fascinating discussion about the historical evidence of what he calls soul-force or Satyagraha. His argument was that soul-force was the basis of the world. Brute-force was an aberration and a break in the even flow of soul-force. It is here that he makes a fundamental difference between Itihas and History. He says that Itihas means: 'It so happened.'[9] On the other hand, for him history means the doings of kings and emperors. He says: 'History, as we know it, is a record of the wars of the world, and so there is a proverb among Englishmen that a nation which has no history, that is no wars, is a happy nation. How kings played, how they became enemies of one another is found accurately recorded in history.'[10] Thus, he makes a crucial distinction between Itihas and history. Itihas is for him a record of things as they happened. History, on the other hand, is a record of wars between kings and emperors. He therefore says that it is impossible for history to record instances of the use of Satyagraha or soul-force. He describes it beautifully; he says, 'You cannot expect silver-ore in a tin mine.'[11] He thus could use the word Itihas in the Gujarati title of the book, but not in English as history was not for him a translation of the term Itihas. Itihas and history were two very different enterprises for him. History could not have recorded the events, which dealt with the advent and the use of soul-force. This shows that for Gandhi translation is a philosophical problem. He was not willing to employ two terms as convertible terms, even if their usage had become customary as for him they represented two divergent traditions.

Let us take another example of this process. If there was a book that altered the course of his life in a definitive way, it was John Ruskin's *Unto This Last*. In the autobiography, he has described how he came under the 'magic spell of the book.' He read this book while on a train journey from Johannesburg to Durban. He has described the impact of the book in the autobiography. 'The book was impossible to lay aside, once I had begun to read it. It gripped me. Johannesburg to Durban was a twenty-four hours' journey. The train reached there in the evening. I could not get any sleep that night. I was determined to change my life in accordance with the ideals of the book.'[12] This book brought about 'instantaneous and practical' transformations in his life. He decided to move to a farm, establish a community there, and live by bread-labour. Not everyone would have been similarly influenced. Gandhi admits that the book by Ruskin reflected some of his own deepest convictions and hence it touched him. He has said this beautifully: 'A poet is one who can call forth the good latent in the human breast. Poets do not influence all alike, for everyone is not evolved in an equal measure.'[13] Gandhi also decided to translate the book into Gujarati. It is not a translation in the usual sense of the term. He rendered into Gujarati a paraphrase of the book. Through the Gujarati paraphrase, he wanted to convey three principles that he had gleaned from the book. These were:

1. That the good of the individual is contained in the good of all.
2. That a lawyer's work has the same value as the barber's, inasmuch as all have the same right to earning their livelihood from their work.
3. That a life of labour, i.e., the life of the tiller of the soil and the handicraftsman, is the life worth living.[14]

In the preface of the translation, he clarifies the purpose further. He wished to present a point of view counter to the utilitarian perspective that it was man's duty to promote the happiness of the greatest numbers. Happiness in this context was taken to be material happiness and economic prosperity. It was also held that if in pursuit of this happiness any moral laws were violated, it does not matter much. India too was in grip of such ideas, which according to Gandhi was the cause of its ruin. He says: 'We in India are much given nowadays to imitation of the West. We do grant that it is necessary to imitate the West in certain respects. At the same time there is no doubt that many western ideas are wrong.'[15] Gandhi wanted to establish with the help of Ruskin's book that quest for material and physical happiness for the majority has no sanction from the divine law. He agreed with Ruskin that one could not pursue happiness in violation of the moral law. Gandhi said in the preface, 'The summary of his work which we offer here is not really a translation. If we translated it, the common reader might be unable to follow some of the Biblical allusions, etc. We present therefore only the substance of Ruskin's work. We do not even explain what the title of the book means, for it be understood only by a person who has read the Bible in English.'[16] The title of Ruskin's book, *Unto This Last* is derived from Christ's parable of the Vineyard; where a man paid equal wages to all labourers regardless of the time they had spent working in his vineyard. When he was asked, he replied: 'I will give unto this last, even as unto thee.' (Mathew xx.1–14) The meaning that both Ruskin and Gandhi derived from this parable was that the relationship between the employer and the employee should not be one of profit or advantage but of justice. Gandhi's transposition of this principle in Gujarati is a sign of his philosophical depth. The phrase Unto This Last would have been translated in Gujarati as *Antyodaya* or the welfare of the last person. Gandhi does not translate it as Antyodaya but as *Sarvodaya*. Sarvodaya means 'welfare of all.' This was the central idea of Gandhi's economic thinking. He believed that a just social order required that each benefit equally. This was possible, he argued, only when people followed moral laws. Observance of morality in this case meant that human beings limit their material wants. If each were to pursue the path of material gain without the consideration of fellow beings, it could result in exploitation and an unjust system. Gandhi's thinking not only influenced the translation of the title as Sarvodaya but other sections also. Ruskin's first chapter is called 'The Roots of Honour'; Gandhi translated it as the 'Roots of Truth.' This again, is based on his philosophy that truth was the foundation of human life. If the principle quest of a human being were truth, it would automatically lead him to a moral path.

We find a similar pattern in his translation of Plato's *Defence of Socrates*. It is significant that Gandhi was translating Ruskin and the *Defence of Socrates* almost simultaneously.[17] The question that we must ask is, why was he doing these translations in this period? Gandhi was engaged in fighting injustice in South Africa. In September of 1906, he had found a new method of protest. This method was called Satyagraha (we will deal with the history of this word and Gandhi's search for its English equivalent a little later); it involved acceptance of suffering for the sake of truth. Gandhi had to convince the Indian community in South Africa, which consisted largely of traders and indentured labour, that it was their duty to undergo suffering even at the cost of their life for the sake of truth and justice. Gandhi was looking for historical figures that had so sacrificed their lives for the sake of truth. Socrates was a natural choice. Gandhi translated—again it was a paraphrase—of Plato's *Defence of Socrates*—for the readers of the *Indian Opinion*. We find the pattern repeating itself. Gandhi called it 'Story of a Soldier of Truth.' Socrates is presented here as someone who laid down his life for truth. In fact, Gandhi calls him a Satyagrahi. He wrote: 'We must learn to live and die like Socrates. He was, moreover, a great Satyagrahi.'[18] He believed that if people out of fear of death or dishonour fail to either realize or examine their shortcomings, India and Indians could never be free. India will have to cleanse itself and emerge pure. The only path of purity for Gandhi was to sacrifice the self. He urges the readers to imbibe the deep sacrifice of Socrates. 'We argued thus and saw in the words of a great soul like Socrates the qualities of an elixir. We wanted our readers, therefore, to imbibe a deep draught of it, so that they might be able to fight—and to help others fight the disease. It is with this objective in mind that we summarize Socrates' speech.'[19]

Thus, Gandhi's translations or paraphrases of Western texts were largely motivated not by literary but philosophical and pedagogic considerations. It was his way of engaging with those aspects of Western philosophical traditions, which echoed his own thoughts.

But this process was not one sided. He was equally concerned with reaching out to the West. He knew that he was engaged not only in a political dialogue with the West but a cultural and a civilizational dialogue as well. Let us elaborate this point.

Gandhi believed that India was subjugated not by the British political power but primarily by modern Western civilization. The modern Western Civilization was for him characterised by a desire to increase bodily comfort and a search of meaning and fulfilment in physical pursuits. He said: 'Its true test lies in the fact that people living in it make bodily welfare the object of life.'[20] This civilization for him was irreligious. He called it a Satanic Civilization and Black Age. A true civilization for him was that mode of conduct, which points to man the path of duty. Performance of duty and observance of morality were convertible terms. Observance of morality was possible only when we attain mastery over our minds and passions. It is by observing morality that we know our selves. Thus, civilization for him opens up the possibility of knowing ourselves.

The other philosophical notion important to understand Gandhi was what he calls the relationship between the means and the ends. He argued that means and ends were inviolably linked with each other. He also argued that it was not sufficient to have ends that were good and moral; the means to that end had also to be equally moral and pure. His lifelong search was to find such moral means. The question before him was how to attain Swaraj, self-rule and what means to employ for that. Many had argued in favour of armed opposition to the British. This was unacceptable to him. He believed that armed opposition or what he described as brute force were peculiar to the West. If India were to employ such means, what it would get would be Western civilization without the British. If Indian civilization was moral, the means adopted had to be moral. In South Africa, he invented a method that came to be known as Satyagraha. Before we go on to the history of the term let us consider what it means. Satyagraha is a method of securing rights by self-suffering. When I refuse to do something that is repugnant to my conscience and accept punishment for disobedience I employ Satyagraha.

This was a new method. It required a word or a term that would capture its essence. Gandhi himself could not come up with the name. When he was in South Africa, he announced a competition for the readers of his weekly the *Indian Opinion* and sought suggestions. His close associate and relative Maganlal Gandhi came up with a term *Sadagraha*. This term was composed of two terms *Sad*, meaning good or virtuous and *Agraha*, meaning insistence. Thus, the term Sadagraha meant insistence for the good and the virtuous.

Gandhi turned Sadagraha into Satyagraha, combining *Sat*, that is Truth and *Agraha*. In the initial phase, Gandhi appeared uncertain about the efficacy and resonance of the term. He was also concerned about its translatability in English. He used four terms as mutually convertible terms. These were Satyagraha, Atmabal that is soul-force, *Dayabal* that is love-force and the English term passive resistance. Sometimes, he and others also used a term associated with Henry David Thoreau. The most peculiar term here is Dayabal or what he called love-force. He is employing the Christian idea of love and compassion and translating that into Gujarati as Daya. Daya in Gujarati and Sanskrit means compassion, Love would be translated as *Prem*. Gandhi instead of translating love as Prem translates it as Daya and expands the meaning of the Gujarati phrase Daya.

His struggle with the term Passive Resistance is indicative of his deep philosophical anxiety to communicate the true essence of a term. He and others around him used the term passive resistance to denote Satyagraha in the initial years. In fact, Gandhi himself used the term passive resistance in his English translation of *Hind Swaraj*. But soon, he began to be dissatisfied and disenchanted with the term passive resistance. He believed that passive resistance was both historically and philosophically different from Satyagraha. He became aware of the problem when a newspaper in Johannesburg described passive resistance as a weapon of the weak. The newspaper wrote: 'The Transvaal Indians have had recourse to passive resistance when all other means of securing redress proved to be of no avail. They do not enjoy the franchise. Numerically, they are only few. They are weak and have no arms. Therefore they have taken recourse to passive resistance which is a weapon of the weak.'[21]

Gandhi says that he was taken by surprise by this description. He soon realised the implications of the term passive resistance.

It implied that if the Indians were numerically stronger, had franchise and arms, they would have taken recourse to some other method and not opted for the 'weapon of the weak.' This forced Gandhi to clarify the distinction between passive resistance and soul-force or Satyagraha. As Gandhi went into the historical incidents associated with passive resistance, the difference between Satyagraha and passive resistance became sharper. He realised that, in the English social and political history, passive resistance was associated with the opposition of numerically weaker and disenfranchised people. Gandhi also realised that in the recent past, non-conformist Christians and women as part of the suffragette movement, had employed passive resistance. He also realised that the non-conformists and the suffragists differed on the question of the use of physical force. The non-conformist would eschew the use of force even if it was a practical proposition, while the suffragists were not averse to the use of certain forms of physical force.

Gandhi was absolutely certain that there was no place for brute force in the movement of the Indian people. No matter how much the Indians suffered, they would never use physical force. Passive resistance implied that when Indians gained in strength and learnt to use arms they would adopt more violent methods of protest. In Gandhi's conception of Satyagraha there was not the slightest possibility of the use of arms. He said: 'Satyagraha is soul force pure and simple, and whenever and to whatever extent there is room for the use of arms or physical force or brute force, there and to that extent is there so much less possibility for soul force.'[22] Gandhi realised that passive resistance and Satyagraha were antagonistic forces. Passive resistance offered the possibility of the use of arms, it could also be offered along with the use of arms. Satyagraha was an act of love according to Gandhi. It could even be offered against the nearest and the dearest but passive resistance could not. Passive resistance did not preclude the possibility to harassing the other party. 'While in Satyagraha there is not the remotest idea of injuring the opponent. Satyagraha postulates the conquest of the adversary by suffering in one's own person.'[23] Gandhi was so convinced of the difference between passive resistance and Satyagraha that he challenged the widely held belief that Jesus Christ was the prince of passive resisters. He said: 'Jesus Christ indeed has been acclaimed as the prince of passive resisters but I submit in that case passive resistance must mean Satyagraha and Satyagraha alone.'[24] Thus, Gandhi decided to use the term Satyagraha both in English and in Gujarati and abandoned the use of the term passive resistance.

Another term that posed such similar philosophical problems was the idea of Swaraj. In the Indian political and social discourse, the term Swaraj was used to denote three overlapping notions. These notions were Home Rule, Independence, and Freedom. It had been used in this sense before Gandhi and even after Gandhi came to dominate the Indian national movement. For Gandhi, Swaraj was none of these. Home Rule meant that Indians should rule in place of the British. Independence was used in the sense of political transfer of power, while freedom implied freedom from slavery. For Gandhi, Swaraj was a much wider notion. In his conception, it had limited political scope. He defined Swaraj as: 'It is Swaraj when we learn to rule ourselves.'[25] To rule one's self meant to have control over the mind and passions, to lead a moral, duty bound life. Swaraj in this sense was a means of self-realisation. If Swaraj was so understood it was not an event or a fact. Independence and Home Rule were events. Freedom entailed a pre supposition of the state of slavery. It was not political slavery that Gandhi was perturbed by. In his conception, Indian was being ground under not the British rule but the modern Western civilization. Those Indians, who were not influenced by this civilization were free. He said: 'The whole of India is not touched. Those alone who have been affected by western civilization have become enslaved.'[26] The moment those who have become enslaved become free of the influence of the Western civilization, India would become free. He faced this difficulty while translating the *Hind Swaraj* into English. He translated the title as *Indian Home Rule*. It was a poor substitute for Swaraj. In fact, in the book he had argued against the desire to have mere Home Rule. Gandhi quickly abandoned the idea of Home Rule. Throughout the translation, he stayed with the term Swaraj in English. The fact that independence, freedom and home rule were not Swaraj for him is also borne out by the fact that after India became independent in 1947, Gandhi called upon the people of India to strive towards real Swaraj and advised that the Indian National Congress too strive for Swaraj.

It was not that Gandhi had philosophical dilemmas translating Indian terms in English. He faced similar difficulties rendering into Gujarati certain key notions of the Western discourse. The following examples illustrate this point. In the *Hind Swaraj* Gandhi had to convey four different notions. These were civilization, modern civilization, reform, and progress. These were notions peculiar to his understanding of the Western civilization. Gandhi found it extremely difficult to convey these notions in Gujarati. In the Gujarati original, he used only one term to convey these separate ideas. The term that he used was *Sudhar* or *Sudharo.* The term Sudhar had two meanings in Gujarati. Sudhar means the good path. Sudharo was also used to denote a process of reform. In this usage also, the idea of adopting the good or the right path were inherent. Despite this, Gandhi used the term Sudharo in all of the above senses. It is in the English translation that the specific sense in which the term Sudhar was used came to be illuminated.

Gandhi had similar difficulty in rendering into English another concept that was central to his life and thought. This was the term *Ahimsa*. Ahimsa is the absence of Himsa, absence of violence and hence Ahimsa was always rendered into English as non-violence. Ahimsa was for Gandhi both a way of life and a means integral to his method of Satyagraha. He had no difficulty in translating Ahimsa as non-violence in the sense of a method. But Ahimsa as a way of life, as a philosophic notion that resonated with the teachings of all major religions of the world, posed certain difficulties. Here Ahimsa could not be used in the narrow sense of non-killing. Ahimsa had to be a positive virtue and not a negative attribute. Gandhi finally resolved the problem by resorting to the Christian term Love. He often translated Ahimsa as love. He used a different approach while dealing with another practice that was central to his life. This was the idea of *brahmacharya.* Brahmacharya has been translated as either celibacy or chastity. We know that celibacy and chastity are not exact equivalent terms. Gandhi also rendered Brahmacharya in this limited sense of leading a celibate life. Gandhi's own practice and thinking about brahmacharya went beyond the notion of celibacy, albeit he continued to emphasise the aspect of celibacy. He came to regard brahmacharya as a mode of knowing the self or realising the truth. As his own thought about brahmacharya became more nuanced, Gandhi began to find celibacy a very limited term. To resolve this difficulty, Gandhi went to the root of the term brahmacharya. *Charya* means conduct. *Brahma* means the ultimate reality or Truth. In its etymological sense, brahmacharya is the conduct adopted in search of truth. Its philosophical implications were immense. Brahmacharya in the sense of celibacy meant only sexual control and abstinence, while at its root it meant conduct that leads to self-realization.

Thus, Gandhi had a complex relationship with language and translation. Language had to convey the philosophical moorings of notions. If language in the act of translation failed to capture the true essence of thought, Gandhi was quick to modify and even abandon the exercise. In this sense, Gandhi was truly a bilingual thinker. Perhaps the best way to read him is to do so simultaneously in two languages.

Source: From Suhrud, Tridip. *Reading Gandhi in Two Tongues and Other Essays*. Shimla: Indian Institute of Advanced Study, 2012, pp. 1–20.

Notes

1. Gandhi, M K, *An Autobiography Or The Story of My Experiments with Truth*, Translated from the original Gujarati by Mahadev Desai (Ahmedabad: Navajivan Press, 1999 reprint), p. 57
2. The CWMG has 100 volumes, the Sampoorna Gandhi Vangmaya has 97 volumes and Gandhi No Akshar Deha has 81 volumes.
3. Gandhi, M K; *Satyagraha In South Africa*, Translated From the Gujarati by Valji Govindji Desai, (Ahmedabad: Navajivan, 2003 reprint), p. 91.
4. Gandhi, M K; *An Autobiography*, p. ix
5. *Ibid.*, pp. ix–x
6. For a history of the text and its English translation, see Tridip Suhrud, *An Autobiography: Or The Story of my Experiments with Truth: A Table of Concordance* (New Delhi: Routledge, 2010).
7. Gandhi, M K, *An Autobiography*, p. x

8. *Ibid.*, pp. x–xi
9. *M K Gandhi's Hind Swaraj*, annotated, translated and edited, Suresh Sharma, Tridip Suhrud, (New Delhi: Orient BlackSwan, 2010), pp. 72–73.
10. *Ibid.*, p. 73
11. *Ibid.*
12. Gandhi, M K; *An Autobiography*, p. 249
13. *Ibid.*, p. 250
14. *Ibid.*
15. *CWMG*, Vol. 8, p. 317, 'Sarvodaya-1'
16. *Ibid.*, pp. 317–318
17. The first part of his translation of the *Defence of Socrates* appeared in the *Indian Opinion* of 4.4.1908, while the first part of *Sarvodaya* was published in the *Indian Opinion* of 16.5.1908.
18. *CWMG*, Vol. 8, p. 247, 'Story of a Soldier of Truth-1'
19. *Ibid.*, p. 248
20. *M K Gandhi's Hind Swaraj*, p. 30
21. Gandhi, M K; *Satyagraha In South Africa*, p. 103
22. *Ibid.*, p. 105
23. *Ibid.*, p. 107
24. *Ibid.*
25. *M K Gandhi's Hind Swaraj*, pp. 59–60
26. *Ibid.*, p. 59